THE UNKNOWN RILKE

FIELD TRANSLATION SERIES 8

Rainer Maria Rilke

THE UNKNOWN RILKE

SELECTED POEMS

Translated by Franz Wright

Introduction by Egon Schwarz

FIELD Translation Series 8

Some of these translations originally appeared in *Cut Bank, Durak, Field, Ironwood, New Honolulu Review, Pocketpal, Poetry Now,* and *The Virginia Quarterly Review.*

The Life of Mary first appeared in *Field,* and was subsequently published, in a limited edition, by *Middle Earth Books,* Cambridge.

Publication of this book was made possible through a grant from the Ohio Arts Council.

Library of Congress Cataloging in Publication Data
  Rilke, Rainer Maria (translated by Franz Wright)
    THE UNKNOWN RILKE
    (The FIELD Translation Series; v. 8)

LC: 83-080681

ISBN: 0-932440-14-2
       0-932440-15-0 (paperback)

CONTENTS

III
from *The Uncollected Poems and Fragments*
   (1906-1926)

INTRODUCTION
by Egon Schwarz

There was a time when lovers of poetry had to learn German for the purpose of reading Rilke. This is no longer necessary because there now exist excellent translations such as this one by Franz Wright. Many of the poems have never been rendered into English; all have been translated with great philological care and poetic strength.

The very fact that the first section is composed of pieces from the *New Poems* written in Paris from 1902 to 1907 attests to the translator's acumen. They introduce Rilke's middle period, his first mature one, characterized by the impact of French culture and above all that of the sculptor Auguste Rodin on whom Rilke was writing a monograph and whose secretary he became. Until then he had written a large amount of prose and poetry, some of it very popular, such as the *Stories of the Good Lord, The Lay of the Love and Death of the Cornet Christopher Rilke* and *The Book of Hours*. But all of these works welled up "from within," carried along by the irrepressible flow of Rilke's rhetoric which he himself had begun to distrust. Of *The Book of Hours* he later said that he could have continued in its vein for the rest of his life. He did not, fortunately, for we would probably not read him if he had. In Paris, facing from close range the example of Baudelaire and his successors, Cézanne and the indefatigable Rodin, Rilke realized that poetry was "work," that it had to do with the world, with attentive observation of "things." Armed with a pencil and a notebook he now roamed through the streets, the parks, the zoo, the museums, and formed into verse what he saw. Needless to say, his method did not exclude expression of his concerns, his most intimate feelings, even his metaphysics. On the contrary, the encounter between the outside world and his inner life for the first time created the balance that poetry needs if it is to last, since reality is too boring, mental phenomena too fleeting, to let them be rewarding subjects of art — separately. No one has described Rilke's fusion of the two more cogently than he himself, for example in the poem "The Spanish Trilogy" (Section 3, p. 104). "The Island" admirably recreates the atmosphere of the North Sea, harsh and melancholy, but it is also a study of loneliness and inwardness. The switch from island to star in the third part may be felt to be a poetic inconsistency by some, but it does reveal the metaphorical nature of Rilke's objects. In other poems, for example "Tombs of the Hetáerae" and "Washing the Corpse," he goes a step farther, forcing the onlooker to see through the appearance of things and to understand their true meaning. In each case a typically Rilkean reversal of vision, a kind of epiphany takes place, that compels us to change our ways. What at first sight seemed ghastly decay suddenly reveals the indestructible unity of life and death.

It is possible that the *New Poems* are less well known than either Rilke's popular early poetry or the two famous cycles of 1922, the *Duino Elegies* and *The Sonnets to Orpheus*, written so close to the poet's death. But it is beginning with the second section, devoted to "The Life of Mary," that the translator really justifies the title he has chosen for this volume, the unknown Rilke. These poems have been neglected by general readers and scholars alike, perhaps because, though published in 1913 when Rilke was in his late thirties, in a way they signify a return to an earlier stage of writing. Heinrich Vogeler, an *art nouveau* painter who had invited Rilke to join the artists' colony of Worpswede in 1900 and introduced him to his future wife Clara, now reminded his friend of an old project for which he was to provide the illustrations and Rilke the text. Somewhat reluctantly and as a favor to Vogeler, Rilke composed twelve more poems in the style of three that stemmed from his Worpswede sojourn. The cycle dwells on significant stations in the life of the Virgin (Annunciation, Birth of Christ, Pietà, etc.) and may thus resemble a more naive stage in Rilke's poetry when he had not yet explicitly renounced the Catholicism of his childhood (as he did for example in his "Letter of a Young Worker" of 1922). But in spite of the seamless combination of the older with the new poems, Rilke could no more turn back the wheel of history than the rest of us. "The Life of Mary" does not and cannot deny the maturing process he had undergone in more than a decade. True to the mode developed in the *New Poems* Rilke continues here to reinterpret myth. What meets the eye or is part of an accepted belief is revealed to contain an essentially different truth. Behind the noumenon appears another reality, the life of a woman and those close to her, whose simple accomplishments are no less miraculous because they are customarily overlooked.

As one can see, Rilke was a non-conformist,

at odds with his age, its technology, its capitalism, particularly its bourgeoisie and what it did to the human soul. This becomes evident from Section III, made up of little known poems from the last two decades of his life, including long fragments that had once been destined to be part of the *Duino Elegies*. What has been said of the *New Poems* holds true also of these: they are emblematic in the sense that the images, themes and titles refer to an outer reality that is merely the "objective correlative" of mental processes and therefore in need of reinterpretation. Rilke takes a fresh look at everything and resurrects what has become conventional or trite to new vibrant life. It should be observed that the later the date of their origin — some were written in Muzot, Rilke's last castle-like retreat in the Swiss Rhone valley — the more visionary they become. Favorite themes such as the transformation of the visible into the invisible, the inexhaustible source of poetry to be found in childhood, the frail human side of religious and mythological figures, the vast significance of early death and, of course, ubiquitously, the redeeming power of art, prevail throughout.

The motto for this volume has been well chosen because what unifies these poems is

Rilke's passionate monism, his refusal to accept the deeply ingrained polarities of our thinking, his burning desire to restore the forgotten oneness of material and spiritual phenomena torn apart by Western civilization under the influence of Christianity and Rationalism, to the detriment of Life.

Translator's Note

Locations and dates of composition for Rilke's uncollected poems and fragments were drawn from *GEDICHTE 1906 BIS 1926: Sammlung der Verstreuten und Nachgelassenen Gedichte aus den Mittleren und Späteren Jahren* (Insel-Verlag), edited by Ernst Zinn with the cooperation of Ruth Sieber-Rilke.

I would like to thank Richard Exner, Stuart Friebert, and David Young for helping me complete this book, and for the indefatigable generosity with which they offered their inspirations and encouragement.

F.W.

Leben und Tod: sie sind im Kerne Eins.

I

from NEW POEMS

DAVID SINGS FOR SAUL

1

King, do you hear how my strings
project the spaces we are moving through:
a bewilderment of stars is streaming past,
and we're falling at last like rain,
and wherever this rain falls things blossom.

Girls you have already known
blossom from the women with their eyes on me;
you can follow the scent of the virgins,
and boys stand pressed, slender
and breathing close to secretive doors.

If only my music could bring it all back!
But drunk on elation it stumbles:
your nights, King, your nights —,
oh how lovely they were, those you enfeebled,
all those bodies, how lovely they were.

I think I can accompany your memory,
because I see what's coming. But from what
        strings
should I pluck the dark groans of their lust?

2

King, you who have known all these things
and who conquer and overshadow me
merely by existing:
come down from the throne, break
the harp you've exhausted!

It is a picked tree:
through limbs which once bore you fruit,
a void shows as though made of the days
still to arrive —, days I hardly recognize.

Let me no longer sleep beside the harp;
look closely at this child's hand:
King, do you think it is still
incapable of reaching the octaves of a body?

3

King, you hoard yourself there in the dark
and still I keep you enthralled.
For behold, my strong song is unbroken,
and the universe around us both grows cold.
Both our hearts, mine orphaned, yours deranged,
hang in the clouds of your fury
fiercely entangled and clenched
into one.

Don't you feel how we're changing each other?
King, King, gravity's turning to spirit.
If we could only hold onto each other,
you to youth, King, I to age,
we'd almost make one circling star.

THE ROSE WINDOW

In there: the indolent tread of their paws
causes a silence in which you are almost entangled;
and just as when, suddenly, one of the cats
pulls somebody's glance, as it strays back and
        forth,

powerfully into its own great eye —
and that glance, as if gripped by a whirlpool,
stays afloat an instant
then goes under, and knows itself no more . . .

when the cat's eye, which looks like it's resting,
opens and shuts with a roar, seizes the glance
and taking it in absorbs it into its red blood — :

So at one time, from the dark of cathedrals,
the enormous rose windows seized someone's
        heart
and tore it into God.

GOD IN THE MIDDLE AGES

And they'd stored him up inside themselves
and they wanted him to be and reign
and finally (to hinder his ascension)
they loaded the cargo and ballast

of their great cathedrals on him.
All he had to do
was move around his limitless numerals
pointing, and like a clock regulate

their work and other daily occupations.
But all at once he started striking
and the people, terrified

by his voice, left him
with his inner mechanisms showing,
and fled before his face.

SAINT SEBASTIAN

He stands like a man reclining — completely
held up there by a magnificent choice. Withdrawn
and self-possessed, like mothers when they nurse,
and involved in himself, like a wreath.

And the arrows arrive: now, and now,
as if they were springing from his groin,
shuddering stiffly at the feathered ends.
Yet he just smiles darkly, undamaged.

Only at one point does his sorrow grow
pronounced, the eyes in naked pain, until
they seem to turn aside from something futile;
as if dismissing with utter contempt
the destroyers of beautiful things.

THE LACE

1

Being human: term for a flickering possession,
existence of a happiness still undemonstrated:
is it inhuman, that a pair of eyes
turned into this small densely woven piece of lace?
Do you want them back?

You, long since vanished, and finally blind —
is all your human joy here inside this thing
where your huge feelings went, as between
stem and bark, miniaturized?

Through a tear in fate, a tiny interstice,
you absented your soul from its own time;
and it is so present here in this light
section of lace, it makes me smile at "usefulness."

2

And if someday all we have done
and all that has happened to us
seems so inferior and strange,
as though there'd been no point
in taking the trouble to outgrow our first pair of
        shoes
just to come to this — . . . Shouldn't this
strip of yellowed lace, this tightly meshed
flowery border of lace suffice
to keep us here? Look: this at least got *done*.

A life was ignored in the process, who knows.
A delight was there, was going to be sacrificed,
and finally at any cost
there would exist this thing, not easier than life
yet *finished* and so lovely, as though it weren't too
        soon
to smile and soar.

BEFORE THE SUMMER RAIN

Abruptly, nobody knows what it is, something's
subtracted from the greenness of the park;
you feel it edging closer to the window
without a sound. But pressing and intense,

out of the woods comes the song of a plover,
someone's Jerome comes to mind:
so much passion and solitude rise
from this single voice, which the downpour

will answer. The walls of the hall
have stepped back with their portraits, as though
they weren't allowed to hear us speak.

The faded tapestries reflect
the undecided light of late afternoons
you felt afraid in when you were a child.

THE KING

The King's sixteen years old.
Sixteen and already a state.
He gazes out, as if from ambush,
past the old men of the council

into the hall and at nothing special
and maybe feels only this:
the chilly clasp fastening his fleece
under his long narrow chin.

The unsigned death sentence
lies in front of him for a long time.
And they think: how he tortures himself.

If they knew him better, they'd realize
he's simply counting to seventy, slowly,
before he signs.

THE ISLAND

North Sea

1

The next high tide will wash away the mud flats'
road, on every side it will look the same;
but out there the little island's
eyes are shut; erratically the dike

surrounds its dwellers, born into
a sleep where they get different
worlds confused, in silence: they hardly ever
    speak,
and every sentence is like an epitaph

for something washed ashore, something alien
that arrives without explanation and then stays.
And so it is with everything their eyes describe

from childhood on: it's not there because of them,
it's all too huge, too ruthless, sent from somewhere
    else,
out of proportion even to their loneliness.

2

As though it lay within a crater
on a moon, each farm's surrounded by a dike
and inside the gardens are all dressed
the same, like orphans, groomed identically

by the storm that brings them up so harshly,
threatening to kill them day in, day out.
And you sit inside those houses, looking
in crooked mirrors at the odd objects

standing on the chests. And one of the sons
steps outside in the evening and draws a single
    chord
from a harmonica, like someone quietly weeping;

he heard it played like that once in a foreign
    harbor.
And out there a tremendous cloud
appears, almost menacing, on the outer dike.

3

Only what's inside is near, the rest is far away.
And this interior, crowded, close, everyday,
crammed with everything and beyond describing.
The island's like a shrunken star

which space ignores and soundlessly demolishes
by its unconscious, terrible immensity
so that, unlighted and unseen,
alone,

and only so that this may one day cease,
dark on its own invented course,
it tries to go on, blindly, outside the scheme
of the planets, suns, and galaxies.

TOMBS OF THE HETAERAE

They lie in their long hair
with brown faces sunk deeply into themselves.
Eyes shut as though overwhelmed by the distance.
Skeletons, mouths, flowers. Inside the mouths
the even teeth like pieces of a pocket chess game
in two tiny ivory rows.
Flowers, yellow pearls, and slender bones,
hands and blouses, faded embroidery
stitched over caved-in hearts. And yet
under those rings, talismans
and eye-blue jewels (for remembering by)
remains the still crypt of a womb,
filled to the roof with petals.
And more yellow pearls, scattered apart —
dishes of fired clay whose concave surfaces
once held their images, green shards
of salve containers which once smelled of
        blossoms,
and the figures of small deities: hearth altars,
the heaven of the hetaerae with its ecstatic gods.

Split girdles, polished scarabs,
little figures with huge genitals,
a laughing mouth, dancers and runners,
gold brooches that could be small bows
for hunting the bird and animal amulets,
long needles, elegant household utensils,
and a round fragment with a red hollow, and on it
like a dark inscription over an entranceway
a horse-team's strutting legs.
Still more flowers, pearls, all scattered,
the bright thighs of a small lyre,
and there between the tucked and mistlike veils,
as if trying to split the shoe's cocoon:
the delicate moth of an ankle bone.

And so they lie, entombed with costly
things, jewels, toys, household items,
obliterated trifles (whatever fell into them)
dark as at the bottom of a river.

And that's what they were, river beds
where in brief rapid waves
(in their rush towards the next life)
the bodies of many young men hurled themselves,
and where torrents of grown men flowed.
And sometimes boys broke from the mountains
of childhood, and came shyly tumbling down

and played with what they found there on the
    ground,
till gripped abruptly by the drop-off in their
    feelings. . .

Then they'd fill with clear shallow water
the entire breadth of their broad course
and set whirlpools going in the deep parts;
and for the first time, reflect the banks
and distant bird cries — , while high overhead
a beautiful land's starry nights
rose in a sky without end.

ORPHEUS, EURYDICE, HERMES

This was the eerie mine of souls.
Like silent silver-ore
they veined its darkness. Between roots
the blood that flows off into humans welled up,
looking dense as porphyry in the dark.
Otherwise, there was no red.

There were cliffs
and unreal forests. Bridges spanning emptiness
and that huge gray blind pool
hanging above its distant floor
like a stormy sky over a landscape.
And between still gentle fields
a pale strip of road unwound.

They came along this road.

In front the slender man in the blue cloak,
mute, impatient, looking straight ahead.
Without chewing, his footsteps ate the road
in big bites; and both his hands hung
heavy and clenched by the pour of his garment
and forgot all about the light lyre,
become like a part of his left hand,
rose tendrils strung in the limbs of an olive.
His mind like two minds.
While his gaze ran ahead, like a dog,
turned, and always came back from the distance
to wait at the next bend — ,
his hearing stayed close, like a scent.
At times it seemed to reach all the way back
to the movements of the two others
who ought to be following the whole way up.
And sometimes it seemed there was nothing be-
        hind him
but the echo of his own steps, the small wind
made by his cloak. And yet
he told himself: they were coming, once;
said it out loud, heard it die away. . .
They *were* coming. Only they were two
who moved with terrible stillness. Had he been
        allowed
to turn around just once (wouldn't that look back
mean the disintegration of this whole work,

still to be accomplished) of course he would have
    seen them,
two dim figures walking silently behind:

the god of journeys and secret tidings,
shining eyes inside the traveler's hood,
the slender wand held out in front of him,
and wings beating in his ankles;
and his left hand held out to: her.

This woman who was loved so much, that from
    one lyre
more mourning came than from women in
    mourning;
that a whole world was made from mourning,
    where
everything was present once again: forest and
    valley
and road and village, field, river, and animal;
and that around this mourning-world, just as
around the other earth, a sun
and a silent star-filled sky wheeled,
a mourning-sky with displaced constellations — :
this woman who was loved so much . . .

But she walked alone, holding the god's hand,
her footsteps hindered by her long graveclothes,

39

faltering, gentle, and without impatience.
She was inside herself, like a great hope,
and never thought of the man who walked ahead
or the road that climbed back toward life.
She was inside herself. And her being dead
filled her like tremendous depth.
As a fruit is filled with its sweetness and darkness
she was filled with her big death, still so new
that it hadn't been fathomed.

She found herself in a resurrected
virginity; her sex closed
like a young flower at nightfall.
And her hands were so weaned from marriage
that she suffered from the light
god's endlessly still guiding touch
as from too great an intimacy.

She was no longer the blond woman
who sometimes echoed in the poet's songs,
no longer the fragrance, the island of their wide
    bed,
and no longer the man's to possess.

She was already loosened like long hair
and surrendered like the rain
and issued like massive provisions.

She was already root.

And when all at once the god stopped
her, and with pain in his voice
spoke the words: he has turned around — ,
she couldn't grasp this and quietly said: who?

But far off, in front of the bright door
stood someone whose face
had grown unrecognizable. He just stood and
    watched,
how on this strip of road through the field
the god of secret tidings, with a heartbroken
    expression,
silently turned to follow the form
already starting back along the same road,
footsteps hindered by long graveclothes,
faltering, gentle, and without impatience.

ALCESTIS

Then the Messenger was suddenly among them,
thrown into the wedding supper, boiling over
     now,
like a new ingredient.
They did not feel it, the drinkers, the god's
clandestine entrance, divinity
clinging to him in the form of a damp cloak,
and he merely seemed to be one of them
as he passed in. However,
halfway through a sentence one of the guests
saw the young lord of the house at the head of the
     table
all at once torn from his place, no longer reclining,
and in every way, with his entire being
mirroring a strangeness that beckoned to him
     terribly.
A minute later, as though the mixture had cleared,
all fell still; at bottom only a sediment
of noise and hushed babble, already redolent
of spoiled and forced laughter.

And then they recognized the slender god,
and as he stood there filled inwardly with mission
and unapproachable — , they almost understood.
Indeed, by the time it was uttered, it was
more than all knowledge, beyond comprehension.
Admetus must die. When? This very hour.

But he'd broken through the shell of his terror,
and put out his hands
to bargain with the god. For a few years,
for one more year of youth,
for months, for weeks, for two or three days,
not even days, for nights, just one,
for one more night, this very night: just this.
The god shook his head, and he began to scream
and screamed and could not stop and screamed —
the way his mother screamed when she gave birth.

And she came up to him, an old woman,
and the father came too, the old father,
and both of them stood there, old, obsolete,
    impotent,
beside the screaming one
who all at once, as though he'd never seen them
that close up, gaped at them, broke off, swallowed,
    and spoke:

Father,
are your dregs so important to you —
if anything they take your appetite away.
Go, dump them out. And you,
old woman, what are you
still doing here: you've given birth.
And he grasped them both like beasts to be
    slaughtered
with one hand. Suddenly he let go
and shoved the old couple away, and beaming with
    new inspiration,
and breathing deep, cried out: Kreon, Kreon!
And nothing else; and nothing but that name.
But over his face came the other
thing he *didn't* say, namelessly waiting, as he
radiantly fixed it on the young, beloved friend
across the cluttered table.
Those old people, what kind of ransom is that,
they're all used up, ruined, almost worthless,
but you, you, in all your beauty —

But then he saw his friend no more. He
remained where he was and what arrived was *she*,
almost a little smaller than he remembered,
fragile and sad in the pale bridal dress.
The others there are nothing but the avenue
of her relentless approach closer and closer — :

(soon
she'll be there, in the arms achingly held out).
And as he waits she speaks; but not to him.
She speaks to the god, and the god hears her out,
and all present hear this at one with the god:

No one can substitute for him. I'm that.
I'm the substitute. No one is finished
as I am. After all what is left
of who I was, here? What matters is I die.
Did she who sent you here neglect to mention
that our bed, waiting inside,
is of the underworld? I have taken my leave.
Leave upon leave.
No one dying will ever take more. Yes, I left
to see all that, buried now, under the one
called my husband, disintegrate, vanish.
So take me: I've already died for him.

And like the sudden shifting of the wind at sea
the god approached, almost like somebody nearing
        a corpse,
and all at once was distant from the husband
to whom he tossed, secretly, with a nod
the hundred lifetimes of this world —
Admetus staggered after the two
reaching out for them like someone dreaming.

They
had already moved to the doorway, around which
women crowded in tears. Then
for one instant, he saw the girl's face, she'd turned
with a smile, bright with hope
that was almost a promise: to come back someday,
grown up, from deep death,
to him, the living —

His hands flew up violently
and covered his face while he sank to his knees,
to keep him from witnessing anything beyond the
    smile.

THE LAST JUDGMENT

Shocked as they were never shocked before,
in no apparent order, many full of holes
or coming apart, they squat there in the ruptured
ochre of their fields, and cling

to the shrouds they've grown fond of.
But angels arrive, bringing oil
to trickle into desiccated sockets
and to place under each armpit

a belonging they'd somehow neglected
to desecrate during a whole lifetime's uproar;
for there it can still get a little warmth,

so that it doesn't chill the Lord's hand
up above, when he gathers it from every side
gently, to see if it's worth anything.

WASHING THE CORPSE

They'd gotten used to him. But
when the kitchen lamp came, burning fitfully
in the dark wake of air, the stranger grew
utterly strange. They scrubbed at his neck,

and since they knew nothing of what brought him
      there,
they put their own version together,
scrubbing all the while. One had to cough
and in the meantime set the heavy sponge

right on his face. Which gave the second one a
      chance
to rest, too. The vinegar dribbled
out of the hard brush; while his hideous
cramped hand tried to indicate to the whole
      household
that he wasn't thirsty anymore.

He made his point. Startled, and rapidly
clearing their throats, they took up the work
where they'd left off, so that on the wallpaper
their humped shadows in the mute patterns

reeled and writhed as though caught in a net,
until they had finished his bath.
The night in the uncurtained window frames
was relentless. And somebody without a name
lay there, nude and immaculate, giving the orders.

ONE OF THE OLD WOMEN

Paris

Sometimes in the evening (you know how that is,
don't you) when they stop abruptly and look back
and nod, and a smile made of nothing but patches
shows from under what's left of their hat . . .

Beside them stands a building
with no end, and they coax you along
with the enigma of their scabs,
with that hat, that wrap and gait.

With the hand, secretly waiting in back of
and under their collar, longing for you:
longing maybe to wrap up your hands
in some piece of paper they've saved.

LULLABY

Someday if I lose you,
how will you sleep without
my whispering above you
like the linden's branches?

Without my lying here
awake and placing words, almost
like eyelids, on your breasts,
your limbs, your lips.

Without my closing you
and leaving you alone with what is yours
like a garden with a mass
of mint-balm and star-anise.

II

THE LIFE OF MARY

THE BIRTH OF MARY

Oh what it must have cost the angels not to
instantly break into song, the way we break into
     tears,
when they already knew: tonight the mother
is born of the child, the One, who will soon appear.

They silenced themselves, in mid-flight, and
     pointed to where
the solitary farm of Joachim lay,
and felt in themselves and in space the pure con-
     densation — ,
but none of them were allowed to go down there.

The two were already beside themselves with
     work.
A neighbor woman, feigning shrewdness, didn't
     know how.
And thoughtfully the old man hushed the mooing
of a dark cow: . . . it was never like this before.

THE PRESENTATION OF MARY IN THE TEMPLE

In order to grasp what she was like at that time,
you must first remember a place in yourself
where pillars do their work; where you can sense
stairways; where precarious arches
span the abyss of a space
which only remained in you because it was built up
from blocks that you can no longer lift
out of yourself without toppling.
When you are ready, when everything in you is
        stone,
wall, door, view, vault — , then try
to tear apart a little, with both hands,
the great curtain you have in front of you:
there high things give off a light
which eclipses your feelings and breath.

Upward, downward, palaces rise above palaces,
broader parapets stream out of parapets
and reappear abruptly, above, on such ledges
that if you look you're seized with vertigo.
Meanwhile the clouds from the incense burners
overcast the area around you; but the farthest
things aim right into you with their rays — ,
and when the light from clear bowls of flames
plays on the slowly approaching robes,
how can you bear it?

But she came through, and raised
her eyes to take all of this in.
(A child, a little girl among women.)
Then quietly and full of self-possession
she mounted toward all this display: it let her
have her way. Because the things men build
were now completely surpassed by the praise
in her heart, and by her desire to
give herself up to what she secretly knew:
her parents fully intended to hand her over,
the menacing one with the jeweled breast
received her, apparently: and she walked right
        through them,
small as she was, moving out of every hand
into her own destiny which was finished now,
higher than the hall, heavier than the house.

THE ANNUNCIATION

It isn't just that an angel entered: realize
this is not what startled her. She might have been
somebody else, and the angel
some sunlight or, at night, the moon
occupying itself in her room — , so quietly
she accustomed herself to the form he took.
She barely suspected that this kind of visit
is exhausting to angels. (Oh if we knew
how pure she was. Didn't a deer,
catching sight of her once in the forest,
lose itself so much in looking at her
that without coupling it conceived the unicorn,
the animal of light, the pure animal!)
It's not just that he walked in, but that
he placed the face of a young man
so close to hers: his gaze and the one
with which she answered it blended
so much, suddenly, that everything else vanished
and what millions saw, built, and endured
crowded inside of her: only her and him:

seeing and seen, eye and whatever is beautiful to
        the eye
nowhere else but right here. *This*
is startling. And it startled them both.

Then the angel sang his song.

THE VISITATION OF MARY

She still moved lightly at first,
though climbing, she was already aware
of her miraculous body — , then
she stood, breathing heavily, on the high

hills of Judea. It was no longer that country
but her abundance that spread all around her;
going on, she felt: no one could ever rise
beyond the greatness she felt now.

And she longed to lay her hand upon
the other body, further along than hers.
And the women swayed toward each other
and touched one another's dress and hair.

Each sheltered herself in her relative,
filled with her holiness.
Ah, the Savior in her was still blossom:
yet even the Baptist inside her cousin's womb
already leaped with delight.

JOSEPH'S SUSPICION

The angel spoke and went to great trouble
over this man with the clenched fists:
Don't you see that in every fold
she is as fresh as God's morning?

The other stared at him darkly,
muttering: Well, what has changed her?
Until the angel cried: Carpenter,
don't you see the Lord's hand in this *yet*?

Because you make boards, are you proud
enough to raise your voice to him
who modestly makes buds and leaves
grow from the same wood?

He understood. And he looked up,
very shaken, to see the angel
who was gone. Then he slowly
pushed off his cap. And sang in praise.

ANNUNCIATION TO THE SHEPHERDS

Look up, friends. Men there by the fire,
men used to searching the unfathomable sky,
star-watchers, come here! Look. I am a new
star rising. My entire being burns
and shines so intensely and is so enormously
full of light that the deep firmament is
no longer enough for me. Let my radiance come
into your lives: oh, the dark looks,
the dark hearts, nocturnal fates
that fill you. Shepherds, how alone I am
in you. All at once I have room.
Don't look so amazed: the huge breadfruit tree
casts a shadow. Yes. Because of me.

Fearless ones, oh if you knew
how in the moment the future shines
on your upturned faces! Much will take place
in this strong light. I open my mind to you
because you do not talk; to you good men
everything here speaks. Rain and fire speak,
passages of birds, the wind and what you are,
no one excels and fattens
on vanity. You never clutch
things to the chest's cavity
in order to torment them. Ecstasy
streams through an angel the same way
the earthly goes through you. And if a thornbush
ignited suddenly, it would be the Eternal One
speaking to you; and if Cherubim
decided to appear walking alongside
your herd, it wouldn't surprise you:
you'd throw yourselves down on your faces
praising, and tell yourselves this is the world.

It was. But now a new thing shall be
and cause the world to move in greater circles.
What is a thornbush to us: God appears
inside a virgin's womb. I am the light
of her ecstasy, guiding you.

THE BIRTH OF CHRIST

If you had lacked the simplicity, how
could this have happened to you, lighting the
    night?
Look: God, who thundered over the people,
makes himself gentle and comes through you into
    the world.

Had you imagined him greater?

What is greatness? His destiny moves in a straight
line through all measurements, crossing them out.
Not even a star has a course like his.
Look how great these kings are, look

how they spread in front of you, your womb,

treasures which they thought the greatest.
And perhaps you are astonished by their gifts — :
But look, again, in the folds of your clothes,
how even now he surpasses all that.

All amber, brought from far off,

all wrought gold and aromatic spices
that moved about, blurred, in your senses:
all of that belonged to one brief hurried moment
and in the end one regrets it . . .

But (you will see): he brings joy.

REST ON THE FLIGHT INTO EGYPT

Having just now flown, out of
breath, from the slaughter of children:
oh how imperceptibly they had grown
great in the course of their journey.

The horror in their timid looks
back over their shoulders had barely disappeared,
and on their gray mule they were already
endangering entire cities;

for as they approached — small in a huge
land, nothing — the strong temples,
the idols broke down as if unmasked
and completely lost their minds.

Is it conceivable that on account of their
passage all things grew so desperately enraged?
And they grew frightened of themselves,
only the child was strangely at ease.

Nevertheless they were forced to
sit down for a while: but, look
what happened: the still tree above them
there, like someone serving:

it bowed. The identical tree
whose garlands preserve the foreheads
of dead pharaohs for all time
bowed. It felt new crowns
blossoming. And they sat as in a dream.

THE MARRIAGE AT CANA

How could she not have been proud of him
who, even at her simplest, made her beautiful?
Even the night, accustomed to greatness,
went beyond itself the moment he appeared.

Didn't his once overstepping himself
add, incomprehensibly, to his glory?
And didn't the wisest exchange their mouths
for their ears? And didn't the house

seem new again holding his voice? Yes,
there must have been hundreds of times
when she had to restrain her delight
from shining on him. She followed him, in awe.

But there at the wedding,
when suddenly the wine ran out,

she glanced across at him, asking for some gesture
without noticing he was unwilling.

Then he did it. She only understood later
that she had rushed him into it:
he'd caused a miracle, it couldn't be
stopped, the course of his life was decided

forever. Yes, it was in writing.
But was it already prepared for?
She: she brought it about
in her vanity's blindness.

She sat at the table covered with fruit
and vegetables, taking part, oblivious
to the fact that the water of her tears
had become blood with this wine.

BEFORE THE PASSION

If this is what you wanted, you shouldn't
have been allowed to spring from a woman's body.
Saviors ought to be mined in the mountains
where the hard is broken from the hard.

Doesn't it trouble you at all to devastate
your lovely valley? Look at my frailty:
I have nothing, only brooks of milk and tears,
and you were always on the strongest side.

How lavishly you were announced to me!
Why didn't you come out of me terribly, all at
        once?
When all you really want are tigers to tear you to
        pieces
why did they bring me up in the women's house

to sew you the pure white clothes
without the slightest trace
of a seam to scratch you — : my whole life was like
        that.
Now all at once you alter nature's course.

PIETA

Now my anguish is complete. It is unspeakable,
it fills me. I am numb
like the stone's core.
I am hard, and know only one thing:
you grew big —
. . . and grew big,
in order to stand outside
my heart, an agony
bigger than it is capable of.
Now you're lying right across my lap,
now I can no longer give you
birth.

QUIETING OF MARY AT THE
RESURRECTION

What they felt at that moment: isn't it
sweeter than any other secret
and at the same time earthly:
the moment he met her, relieved, still
a little pale from the grave:
every part of him risen.
Met her first! It would be impossible
to say how much it healed them.
Yes, they were healing, that's all. Without even
        having to
touch each other very hard.
For hardly a second he
laid his almost
eternal hand on her woman's shoulder.
And quietly
like the trees when spring comes,
endlessly at one,
they began this season
of their ultimate intimacy.

THE DEATH OF MARY

1

The identical angel, the great one who
once brought down the news of her conception
stood there, waiting for her to notice him
and said: It is now time for you to appear.
And as before she was startled and thereby proved
herself the maiden, deeply confirming what he
    knew.
Then he grew radiant and stepped so near
he disappeared into her face — and summoned
the apostles who'd gone out in every direction
to gather again in the house on the slope,
the house of the last supper. They came, this time
it was harder, and entered in fear: she lay
there in the narrow bed, weirdly immersed
in her election and in her dying,
completely intact, like one unused
in life, tuned to angelic song.

Only when she noticed them waiting behind
their candles, she tore herself from
the excess of voices and out of her heart
she gave away the two dresses she owned,
and raised her eyes to them one at a time . . .
(oh source of incomprehensible streams of tears).

But she lay back again in her weariness
drawing the sky down so near to Jerusalem
that to step outside her soul
had only to stretch a little: even now
the one who knew her life so well
was lifting her into her own divinity.

2

Who would have thought that before her coming
the myriad heavens were still incomplete?
The resurrected one had taken his seat
but the seat beside him had been vacant
for twenty-four years. They had already
begun to get used to that pure omission
that was as if healed over, filled by the son's
overflowing of light.

And so the moment she stepped into heaven,
as much as she longed to, she didn't approach him:
there was no room, only he was there, giving
a radiance that hurt her eyes.
Yet as her groping form
went in among the newly blessed
and took her place inconspicuously, light
among light, there broke from her the repression
of so much light that angels illuminated
by her cried out in awe: Who is *she*?
Utter astonishment. Then they all saw
how God the Father eclipsed our Lord
so that surrounded by a gentle dusk
the empty place grew visible, like
some small sadness, a sign of loneliness,
something he still endured, a residue
of earthly time, a partially healed wound.

They looked to her: leaning ahead, she looked
at him anxiously, as if to say: I am
his longest suffering. And suddenly she pitched
    forward.
But the angels lifted her up, supported her
and singing carried her that last few feet in the air.

3

Then an angel appeared before the Apostle
Thomas, who'd arrived too late — , a swift
angel prepared for this long in advance
who commanded, at the grave:

Move the stone aside. Do you want to know
where she is, the one who moved your heart?
Look: she was placed in there for a while
like a pillow of lavender

so that in the future the earth
would smell of her in its folds, like her clothes.
Everything dead (you must feel it), everything sick
is numbed by her good fragrance.

Look at the shroud: where is the bleaching ground
where it would be made to shine and not shrink?
The light from her pure corpse
purified it more than the sunlight.

Doesn't it astonish you, how gently she took leave
    of it.
It's as if she was still in it, nothing has been
    touched.
And yet above us the heavens are torn!
Friend, kneel here. Look after me when I go, and
    sing.

III

FROM THE UNCOLLECTED POEMS
AND FRAGMENTS
(1906-1926)

IMPROVISATIONS OF THE CAPRISIAN WINTER

1

Every day you stand there towering in the heart's
presence, mountain, stone,
wilderness, impasse: God, in whom I climb
and descend all alone and lose the way . . .,
retracing my steps day after day.
Sometimes at a crossroads the wind shows me a
        direction,
makes me pitch forward at a path's source,
or some road absorbs me into the silence.
But your unseen design
constricts the roads like alum,
until they resemble old wandering furrows
and lose themselves in gray chasms . . .

Oh let me, let me with my eyes
closed, like eyes that have swallowed themselves,
pause with my back to these colossi
until the vertigo passes
and my transported senses return to their places.
Is everything inside me really shifting?
Is nothing solid there,
nothing rooted by the right
to its own gravity? My most terrified and my
        best . . .
swept away effortlessly by the whirlwind
into the depths . . .

Face, my face:
whose are you? what
are you the face of?
How can you serve as face for such insides,
where beginning and decomposition
ceaselessly converge.
Does the forest have a face?
Doesn't the great basalt mountain
stand there without a face?
Doesn't the sea
rise facelessly
from the abyss of the sea?
Isn't the sky mirrored in it
without brow, without mouth, without chin?

Doesn't one of the animals sometimes approach
as though it were pleading: take my face?
Their faces are too hard for them
and hold what little soul they have
much too far into the world. And we?
Animals of the soul, bewildered
by all that's inside us, unprepared
for anything, grazing
souls,
don't we pass whole nights
pleading with the power that hears
for the nonface
which belongs to the darkness in us.

Darkness, my darkness, I stand here with you,
and everything passes outside;
and all I ask is a voice like an animal's,
one voice, a single cry
for all — . Because what good to me
are the innumerable words that come and go,
when the cry of a bird,
uttered again and again,
makes a tiny heart so vast and one
with the heart of the air, the heart of the grove,
and so radiantly audible to Him . . . :
who again and again, with every dawn,
ascends: most precipitous stone.

Even if I pile my heart on top of my mind and add
my loneliness and my longing:
how small it remains,
because *He* towers beyond it.

2

What if I found again, among hundreds of things:
my heart, the overburdened heart, still alive, and
          took it
again into my hands, finding it among
so many things, my heart:
and lifted it into the outer
world, into gray morning rain,
into the day which incessantly wanders
and reflects on the long roads;
or at dusk, into the night, that clear
act of mercy approaching . . .

And held it up, as far as I am able,
into wind and stillness;
when I no longer can
would you take it then?
Oh take it, plant it! No,
just hurl it down on the cliffs, on granite, wherever
it might land; as soon
as it has fallen from your hands
it will grow all by itself, will take

clutching root in the hardest of all
mountains, one the seasons cannot reach.
And if it fails to grow, if it isn't young enough,
from the mountain it will slowly learn
its kind, and learn its color from the stone,
and lie there underneath its shards of rock,
become one with the mountain
and crumble with it
and reach with it into the storm.

And if you wish it to settle at the bottom
of the mute sea, among shells,
who knows if from its fluted mouth
an animal won't emerge, one that tries to seize you
with its rays and pull you in
and sleep with you.

. . . just let it find
a spot somewhere and not be
so in space, which your stars
barely fill. See how it falls through space.

Nobody expects you to hold it like animals'
hearts, in your hand day and night;
if only it could rest there for a while!
Once you abandoned the hearts
of your saints in the most desperate hovels,

and still they flourished there and brought you
      profit.

     . . . .

You strange uncontrollable squanderer,
you sweep right past me in full leap. You splendid
stag! You ancient stag with your hundred antlers!
Again and again you shed them
from your head and lightly fly right through
your hunters (see how everything
supports and bears you on!) —
and all they see — oh wild, unbridled! —
is how the world slams shut behind you.

3

So many things lie torn open
by rash hands that arrived too late,
in search of you: they wanted to know.

And sometimes in an old book
an incomprehensible passage is underlined.
You were there, once. What has become of you?

If somebody held you, you broke him,
his heart remained open, and you weren't inside;
if anyone ever addressed you,
it was with a breathless: Where are you going?

It happened to me, too. Except I asked nothing of
        you.
I simply serve, and have no case to plead.
Waiting patiently, I hold the willing glance
of my face in the wind of the days
and never complain to the nights . . .
                                    (because I see they know)

4

Now close your eyes: so that now
we may enfold all this
inside our darkness, inside our peace,
(as if it were ours).
Among wishes, and sketches,
among unfinished things
that we'll finish someday,
somewhere inside us, deep down
this too exists now; it's like a letter
that we seal.

Keep your eyes closed. It isn't *there*,
nothing is there, only night;
the night's room around a little light,
(you know it well).
But this is all *inside* you now, awake —
and bears along your soft closed face
like a stream . . .

And now bears you along. And everything inside
      you,
and you are laid like a rose petal
on your soul, which is rising.
Why does it mean so much to us: to *see*?
To stand at the edge of that cliff?
Whom did we have in mind, when we welcomed
      that,
spread out before us? . . .
                              Yes, what was it, do you know?

Close your eyes more ardently and recognize
it once again: sea after sea,
heavy with itself, blue from within
and empty at the edges with a sediment of green.
(Which green? No green like this exists any-
      where . . .)
And all at once, breathlessly, cliffs rise
up from it, from so far below they
really cannot tell in their steep ascent how
their ascent might ever cease. Suddenly it breaks
      off
right at the sky, there, where it is dense
from too much sky. And beyond, look,
sky again, and on and on
into that immeasurable space: where does sky end?
Don't both those crags radiate sky?

Doesn't its light paint the most distant white, the
        snow,
which appears to be moving and takes our eyes
        with it
into the distances. And it never ceases
being sky, until we breathe it.

Close, close fast your eyes.

Was it this?
You scarcely know. You can no longer distinguish
        it
from what's within you, now.
It's hard to recognize the sky
inside.
The heart moves on and on and never looks.

And yet, as you know, we can close like this
at dusk — like the anemone enfolding
all that happened in a day and opening
a little bigger in the morning.
And to do so isn't just permitted
us, it is expected: learning to close
over the infinite.

(Did you notice the shepherd today? He doesn't
        close.

How could he? The day
flows into him and flows back out again
as from a mask, behind which all is black . . .)

But we may close, securely
close, and among those dark things
that have been inside us for so long, still
house what remains of the inconceivable,
as if it were ours.

"TO DRINK THINGS DISSOLVED
AND DILUTED . . . "

To drink things dissolved and diluted
with eyes used to looking through books
instead of chewing on the kernel of reality

AUTUMN EVENING

Wind from the moon,
abrupt shudder of trees
and a leaf drifting down, groping.
Through the in-between spaces
of feeble street lamps
the distance's dark landscape forces its way
into the flickering city.

THE SICK CHILD

With a slight turn of the head on the pillow
his face returned to the room and observed
the state of things: they were still there.
And it occurred to him: this is all we know.

Yet even of this you could never be sure,
as you lay there for days on end, staring, half
        conscious:
one thing took shape while another dissolved.
        Vagueness
rose from the mirror. But where was that

in whose presence you could always be consoled?
When, at times, even your own hand smelled
unfamiliar, and from the next room
the beloved voices sounded like company.

WALK AT NIGHT

Nothing is *like* something else. What is not wholly
alone with itself, what thing can really be
    expressed?
We name nothing. All we can do
is tolerate, acquaint ourselves
with a single fact: here a sudden brilliance
or there a glimpse momentarily grazes us
as if it were precisely *that* in which resides
what our life is. Whoever resists
will have no world. Whoever grasps too much
will overlook the infinite. Meanwhile,
during such huge nights we are out of danger,
distributed in equal, almost weightless
parts among the stars. How they urge us on.

"OH IN CHILDHOOD, GOD,
HOW EASY YOU WERE . . . "

Oh in childhood, God, how easy you were:
you, whom I cannot take hold of now, anywhere.
One smiled on the things one loved to have around;
they came half way: and you were already in
    reach.
And now, my God, where should I travel to find
    you?
Where do I enter? What mountain must I climb?
If someone asks for you: where should I point?
Where is your rustling grove? Where does your
    animal wander?
Where am I to find the fresh water to wash
my face and sex: I have never been clean.
Where do you reduce the holy things to ash
with the fiery radiance of your eye?
Doesn't the scent of all our depravities

incite your rage? What are you waiting for?
Why don't you change the ravenous to fasters
and hurl an angel at them
until they writhe in their own blood?
Lord, do not be good: be lordly — , refute
the hearsay of their praise:
tear down the house, destroy the bridge,
unleash monstrosities
in the path of those who try to flee.

For we're so enslaved to contemptible needs
we go on believing in, year after year —
if someone holds out their hands to us,
we think *that's* what God is. You red night of
    agony,
you fire-lit sky, you war, you hunger: kill:
for you are the danger we're in.

Not until we place our dying in you
once again, and not simply our preservation,
will everything be yours: solitude and intercourse,
defeat and exaltation.
For the peace you finally bring to come into the
    world,
first you must fall on us, ambush us, tear us limb
    from limb;
for nothing has the power to so utterly destroy
as the way you use us, when you want to set us free.

"OH HAVEN'T YOU KNOWN
NIGHTS OF LOVE . . . "

Oh haven't you known nights of love? Don't
the petals of soft words float upon your blood?
Aren't there places on your dear body
which remember, like a face?

TO LOU ANDREAS-SALOME

1

I kept myself immensely open, yet forgot
that out there more than things exist, or animals
completely at home in themselves, with eyes
which no more reach beyond their life's cir-
       cumference
than pictures in a frame; forgot that always
and in everything I did, I kept stuffing
glimpses into myself: glimpses, opinions, mere
       curiosity.
   Who knows but that eyes take shape in space
and sleep together. Oh, only when my face
is streaming toward you does it cease
being on exhibit, becomes one with yours and
       darkly goes on
and on into your impregnable heart . . .

2

The way someone holds a cloth to stopped breath,
no: the way it is pressed on a wound
from which life wants to come out, in one gush,
unceasingly, I held you to me: I saw

I was getting you red. How could they know
what happened between us? We made up for
    everything
there never was time for. I ripened strangely
at every impulse of omitted youth,
and you, my love, somehow laid down
wildest childhood over my heart!

3

Remembering's just not enough, there
must remain, of those moments, some pure
being in my deepest place, a precipitation
of that immensely oversaturated solution.
For I do not *remember* — , what I *am*
moves me for your sake. I don't pretend you're
    there
at desolate places where it's getting cold now,
places you've moved on from: even your not being
    there
still holds your warmth and is more real and more
than a deprivation. Too often
longing misses the point. Why should I cast myself
    out,
when perhaps your influence is a simple thing
to me, like moonlight at a spot by the
    window . . .

THE RAISING OF LAZARUS

Evidently, this was needed. Because people need
to be screamed at with proof.
Still, he imagined Martha and Mary
standing beside him. They would
believe he *could* do it. But no one believed,
every one of them said: Lord,
you come too late.
And he went with them to do what is not done
to nature, in its sleep.
In anger. His eyes half closed,
he asked them the way to the grave. He wept.
A few thought they noticed his tears,
and out of sheer curiosity hurried behind.
Even to walk the road there seemed monstrous
to him, an enactment, a test!

A high fever erupted inside him, contempt
for their insistence on what they called
their Death — , their Being Alive.
And loathing flooded his body
when he hoarsely cried: Move the stone!
By now he must stink, someone suggested
(he'd already lain there four days) — but he
stood it, erect, filled with that gesture
which rose through him, ponderously
raising his hand (a hand never lifted
itself so slowly, or more)
to its full height, shining
an instant in air . . . then clenching
in on itself, abruptly, like a claw, aghast
at the thought *all* the dead might return
from that tomb, where the enormous cocoon of
the corpse was beginning to stir.
But finally, only the one decrepit figure appeared
at the entrance — and they saw
how their vague and inaccurate
life made room for him once more.

THE SPANISH TRILOGY

1

From this cloud, look: so wildly concealing
the star that was there just a moment ago — (and
     from me),
from the moutainous country out there, with its
     night
and the winds of its night, for a while — (and me),
from this valley's river, which catches
the light of clearings torn in the sky — (and me);
to make from me and all of this
one thing, Lord: from me and the sensation
with which the flock, returned to its pen,
accepts and exhales the world's great dark
no longer being there — , me and the light
burning in the gloom of many houses, Lord:
to make one thing; from the strangers,
for I don't know anyone, Lord, and from me,
to make One Thing; from the sleeping,
from unknown old men in some shelter
coughing gravely in their beds, from
children drunk with sleep upon so strange a breast,
from so much uncertainty, and always me,
from me alone and all that I don't know,

to make one thing, Lord Lord Lord, one thing —
heavy with world, like a meteor
whose heaviness is only an accumulating
flight: weighing nothing but its arrival.

2

Why must one go away and take on unfamiliar
        things
like this, just as the bearer of a market basket
mysteriously more and more filled up,
carries it from stand to stand, and ladened down
        continues on
and can never say: Lord, why the banquet?

Why must he stand there like a shepherd,
so abandoned to excessive powers,
taking part so much inside this busy space
that propped against one of the trees of the
        landscape
he'd possess his destiny without so much as
        stirring.
Without even having, in a view too immense,
the comfort of the herd. He has nothing
but world, world the second he looks up,
world at every turn. What others would happily
        own
blindly, uninhabitably penetrates his blood
like music, changing as it flows.

He gets up at night and already has
the cry of a bird in his being
and feels audacious, since he takes the whole
    starry night
into his face, with an effort — oh not like one
busy preparing the night for his love,
lavishing on her the skies he has felt.

3

When I again have the city's congestion
and the inextricable noise and confusion
of traffic all around, may it come to me, apart
from and above all that dense agitation:
the remembered sky and the earthen ridge,
from behind which the flock appeared on its way
    home.
May my mood be of stone, and the shepherd's
day-to-day work seem conceivable to me,
as he advances, and tans, and with the toss of a rock
hems in his flock wherever it's frayed.
Ponderous footsteps, not easy, body deep in thought—
but how splendid he is when he stands! A god
could secretly take on this form
even now, without being diminished.
He lingers now and then moves on, like day itself,

and cloud-shadows pass
through him, like thoughts
the sky is slowly thinking in his place . . .

Whatever, shepherd or god. I place myself in him
like the flickering night-light inside the lamp's
    casing.
The gleam grows still. Death
should have little trouble finding the way.

"IN IGNORANCE BEFORE THE HEAVENS OF MY LIFE . . . "

In ignorance before the heavens of my life,
I stand amazed. Oh enormous stars.
Unfolding and descent. How still.
As if I weren't there. Do I take part in this? Did
I dispense with their pure influence? Do the tides
in my blood rise and fall in consonance with them?
I'll put away wishes, all forms of relationship,
and accustom my heart to its farthest reaches.
It does best to live among its terrifying stars,
and not in apparent protection, pacified by what's
     near.

CHRIST'S DESCENT INTO HELL

When it was too much, he passed out
of the body's unspeakable suffering. Rose. Stepped
    away.
Left alone, the darkness grew afraid
and hurled its bats
at the pale thing — twilight still reeling
with their dread of colliding
against this frozen torment. Dark, restless
air grew discouraged over the corpse; and the
    strong
and watchful animals of night felt all at once hol-
    low, reluctant to move.
Maybe his just-released ghost chose to pause
    there,
near him, in the world. Because the event of his
anguish was still enough.

Nocturnal life struck him as gentle,
and like a mourning space he reached out beyond
    it.
But the earth, parched from the thirst of his
    wounds,
ripped open below him unleashing its shrieks.
He, knower of tortures, heard all hell
scream out and demand to know
if it was over yet: apparently they thought they
    saw
in the fulfillment of his (infinite) pain
the end of their own. And he plunged in,
his spirit did, with the full weight
of the body's exhaustion: moving urgently
through the startled eyes of the grazing shades,
he hurriedly lifted his eyes to meet Adam's,
hurried down, faded, appeared, and vanished in his
    fall
to more appalling depths. Suddenly (higher,
    higher)
suspended right over the middle of the boiling
    screams,
he stepped forth from the tall
tower of his perseverance: without breathing,
stood there, without a railing, landlord of agony.
    Silent.

"ABANDONED IN THE MOUNTAINS OF THE HEART . . . "

Abandoned in the mountains of the heart. Look,
        there, how small,
the last outpost of words, and up higher,
though also very tiny, one last
farmstead of consciousness. Recognize it?
Abandoned in the mountains of the heart. The
        stony ground
under the hands. Yes, a few things still grow
here; at mute precipices
grows an ignorant weed singing out.
And the one who knows? Ah, who began to know,
        and now
is silent, abandoned in the mountains of the heart.
Many walk here, yes, intelligence intact,
all around, many alert mountain creatures
moving on or lingering. And some great confident
        bird
is circling the peaks of unqualified renunciation.
        — But
here, exposed on the mountains of the heart . . .

TO BENVENUTA

Ah, I passed like a wind through their foliage,
I rose away from every house like smoke.
Where others were busy about their routines
I held on like some strange habit.
Easily startled my hands shrank
from the fateful joining with other hands;
all of them, all, hastened my emptying:
and all I could do was be spilled.

You see, even to look at a star
requires some small earthly base,
for confidence can only come from confidence,
everything done well is something done *again*;
ah, night asked so little of me,
and if I did in fact turn to the stars —
the damaged facing the intact — :
What did I stand on? Was I here?

Does the warm course of your heart
rush toward me on this cheerless journey?
Now it's only a matter of hours, and I will
lightly place my hands in yours.
How long they have gone without rest.
Can you imagine, then, what it must mean to me,
traveling like this for years — a stranger among
        strangers —
that now, at last, you're going to take me home.

"THE WAY WATER SURFACES
SILENTLY . . . "

The way water surfaces silently
evaporate, I'm on my knees
to give you my ascending
changing face.

DEATH

Death stands there, a bluish concoction
in a saucerless cup.
Curious place for a cup:
it stands on the back of a hand. You recognize,
only too well, the spot where the handle broke off
on its glassy curve. Dusty. And "Hope"
in exhausted letters on its side.

That's what whoever the drink was prepared for
read off it at some remote breakfast.

What kind of creatures are they, who
finally have to be scared off with poison?

Would they ever leave otherwise? Are they so
    crazy
about these meals made of nothing but obstacle?
You have to remove the difficult present
from them, like a set of false teeth.
Then they start to babble. Babble, babble . . .

. . . .

O falling stars,
glimpsed once from a bridge — :
not to forget this. To last!

REQUIEM ON THE DEATH OF A BOY

What was the point of learning names
and knowing, now, for so long
and from so far away, dog, cow, elephant,
and then the zebra — , what in heaven for?
   The one who's carrying me now
rises like a tide
over all that. Is that what peace is,
to know you once existed, if you failed
to penetrate through hard and gentle alike
and reach the understanding face?

And these beginning hands —

You used to say: he promised . . .
Yes, I promised, only what I promised *you*,
that doesn't scare me anymore.
Sometimes, right by the house, I sat a long time
and looked at a bird.
If only I could have turned into that — looking!
It carried me, it lifted me, my eyebrows
could rise no higher. I loved no one.
It hurt to love — , do you understand, then
I wasn't us
and was much bigger than a man
and was
as if I myself were the threat
and inside of it
I was the seed.

A little seed; I let the street, the wind
enjoy it . . . I let it go.
Because our all sitting together like that
is something I never believed. Cross my heart.
You talked, you laughed, and yet no one was there,
not in the talk, not in the laughter. No.
The glass of wine, the sugar bowl,
they never wavered like you did.
The apple simply lay there. How good that some-
        times was,
to take hold of the big solid apple,

116

the sturdy table, the still breakfast cups,
so kindly — , how they reassured that year.
And sometimes my toys were nice to me, too.
They were almost as reliable
as the other things; only not so peaceful.
They stood there as though on guard,
between me and my hat.
There was a horse made of wood, there was a
        rooster,
there was the doll with only one leg;
I've done a lot for them.
Made the sky small when they stared at it — ,
because I grasped early on: how alone
a wooden horse is. That somebody can make one:
a horse of wood in any size.
It's painted, and later you drag it around,
and on the real road it gets knocked down.
Why wasn't that a lie, when you
called it a "horse"? Because you felt yourself
a little like a horse, maned, muscular,
four-legged (in order to turn someday
into a man)? But at the same time
didn't you feel a bit wooden, for its sake —
turning hard in the quiet,
making less of a face?

Now I almost believe we were gradually switch-
   ing places.
If I looked at a stream, how I would rush by;
if the stream rushed by, I raced to be near it.
Wherever I *saw* a sound, I rang,
and wherever it rang, I was the reason.

And so I pushed myself on everything.
And everything was better off without me,
and became sadder weighted down with me.
   Now I am suddenly parted.
Is this another question, a new lesson?
Or has the time come to explain
the way things are with you? — I worry about
   that.
The house? I never quite knew my way around it.
The rooms? There was so much crammed into
   them.
. . . And mother, who was the dog
really?
And even when we found the berries in the woods,
that seems like such a strange event to me . . .

. . . .

There must be other dead children
to come and play with me. There were
some dying all the time. First lay there in the room,
like I did, and didn't get well.

"Well . . ." How strange that sounds here.
        Does it still mean anything?
Where I am, I think
nobody is sick.
It's already been so long since my sore throat —

Here everyone's like a cool drink.

The ones who're drinking us, I have yet to
        see . . .

. . . .

THE DEATH OF MOSES

None of them were willing, just the dark
defeated angel; choosing a weapon, he cruelly
        approached
the commanded one. But even he
went clanging backward, upward,
and screamed into the heavens: I can't!

For through the thicket of his brow, Moses
had patiently noticed him and gone on writing:
words of blessing and the infinite Name. And his
        eyes
were clear right to the bottom of his powers.

So the Lord, dragging half of the heavens behind
        him,
came hurling down in person and made up a bed
        from the mountain;
laid the old man out. From its orderly dwelling
he summoned the soul; and spoke of much they had
        shared
in the course of an immeasurable friendship.

But finally the soul was satisfied. Admitted
enough had been done, it was finished. Then the
        old
God slowly lowered down over the old
man his ancient face. Drew him out with a kiss

and into his own older age. And with the hands of
        creation
he closed the mountain again. So it would be like
        one,
one created all over again among the mountains of
        earth,
hidden to us.

THE LORD'S WORDS TO JOHN ON PATMOS

Behold: (for no tree shall distract you)
on this island stands nothing but space.
Birds? Be prepared for lions
flying through the air.
Trees would be afraid,
and I do not wish them to see.

But you shall see, perceive, and be
a seer like no man has ever been.
You shall take, grasp, read,
you shall devour my sky's round fruit
which I break in two for you.
That the juice may drip into your eyes,
you shall kneel down with raised head:
for this I sought you out.

And shall write, without looking at what you have
    written;
for this too is urgent: write.
Lay your right hand to the right of the stone
and your left to the left: that I may move them
    both.

And for once I'll be completely present.

  For millions of years I had to hold back
because worlds pass away so slowly,
had again and still again to give,
piecemeal, of my own incandescence
to those gone out
instead of being all heat, to them all.
And so I'm never wholly in Creation:
scarcely have the people received hints of my
    presence
when the stone remembers me no more.

For once I am going to disarm in your presence.
My robes, the garments of my kingdom,
my armor: put aside everything that binds me,
and deprive the tall two-handed sword
the angels wield for me
of my right hand's might. But for now
behold the meaning of my dress:

although We made such splendid garments for
ourself,
nakedness comes in the end.

Satan has servants to bludgeon
whatever grows with most fragility,
and so for a while yet I must
support man in the image he has come to
understand;
but I think I will stir up my beasts:
because there is this yearning in my works
for incessant metamorphosis.

Humans are attached to concepts
they were long in fathoming.
So for a while, let ships be ships
and houses houses.
And the chair, the table, cupboard, chest
and hat, and coat and shoe —
let them remain as they are:
but these forms are not mine.

Whenever they cry out that I am mad,
I'm happy to send down my fire
over those who have.
I like to test one of their things,
to see if I could possibly conceive it — :
if it catches fire it's real.

If man only knew what most delights
an angel's soul, like a waterfall pouring
down constantly over my oldest
commandments — . . . Long ago I should have
withdrawn things like camels and hacked them to
        pieces.
Civilization is not my concern
for I am the rain of fire
and my glance is jagged like the lightning.

Behold I will not suffer one man to remain.
Write:
through the body's dust
I hurl men toward the target
toward labor or toward women
and I need women like I need the leaves.
Only in the child do I pause a moment
for the spreading roar
to gather in its shell-like ear.
Behold, in this small narrow place prepared for
        me, I strike
order into the chaos of my worlds:
what perishes takes place there first.

UNFINISHED ELEGY

Don't let your fate change your mind
about childhood, this indescribable
faithfulness of the divine. Even the prisoner,
left to decay in the dark of his cell,
is secretly nourished by it right to the end.
Timelessly it takes the heart into its keeping.
Even the sick man, who stares out
into space and understands (the room
no longer answers, for it can still recover) —
    curable,
his belongings surround him, feverish, sick along
    with him,
but still curable, all around the lost one — : even he
benefits from childhood. It preserves
incorruptibly, in fallen nature, its affectionate
    space.
Which is not to say it is harmless; that charming lie
which frills and dresses it up could only deceive for
    a while.

126

Nor is it ever safer than we are, or better prepared;
no god counterbalances its weight. It's vulnerable
as we are, as animals in winter are vulnerable.
Even more so: it has no hiding place. Vulnerable,
as if *it* were the threat. Vulnerable
as fire, as a deformed thing, a poison, as whatever
      prowls
at night around the suspicious house, when the
      doors are bolted.
Is there anyone who hasn't noticed the protectors'
      hands
lying, those protective hands — , themselves in so
      much danger:
Then who can do it?
" . . . I!" — What I? — "I, Mother, I can.
                              I was before the world.
The earth has let me in on it, how it comes forth
      with the seed,
that it is one. Oh evenings of confidence, both of us
      rained,
soft and May-like, the earth and I in our womb.
Male! how could you know how deeply at one
we were. The silence of the universe
will never be divulged to *you* the way it closes
      around a growing thing . . ."

Generosity of mothers, voice of those who nurse
    — , and yet!
What you are saying *is* the threat, the whole
unmitigated menace of the world — , and so it
    reverts to "protection,"
and with relief and emotion you feel it.
The intenseness of being a child exists in you
like a center, emptying you of fear, unafraid.

But the fear! It comes to you abruptly
in the end: that's how humans are made,
porous, permeable. A draft
makes its way in through the cracks.
That's fear. From behind
it sneaks up on the child at play, and hisses
indecision in his blood — , the abrupt suspicion
that later on there would be nothing but parts,
    nothing
but a piece, five pieces, and none of them
ever connectable, and all, all fragile.
And already fear's splitting off
through the spine, that forking
branch of desire, turning wooden, a doubting
bough on the Judas-Tree of choice.
Now it's corrupting the doll, the good, the ever
gentle toy, till even as it's being hugged it already
strangely terrifies — . Not in itself,
not with its poor pardonable strangeness,

128

no: with the affection of the child
himself, with all that he agreed to.
Agreed to during those long hours
of trust, the innumerable
hours of confiding play,
when the child measured himself
against and distinguished himself from the You
unselfishly created over there . . .
and experienced to his surprise —
with his strength divided in two —
his own reserve of energy constantly renewed.

Distances of play!
It extended its benefits out past its happy inventor,
into the most recent generation at least,
way past the grandchild . . . optimistic nature!
Death's pretty friend, who through an effortless
      change
outgrew it so many times . . . O doll,
most remote figure — , as stars
learn from enormous abandonment
how to become worlds of their own,
you fashion a star from a child. Is it
too small for the universe? Then you extend
space of feeling between you, that heightened
      space . . .

But suddenly it happens . . .What? When? —
                    Unnameable — rupture —
What? . . . the betrayal . . . half filled with
     existence the doll
refuses to go on existing, says no, doesn't recog-
     nize you.
Stares with averted eyes, just lies
there, knows nothing; not
one more thing — look, how the things
are embarrassed for it,

. . . .

THE HAND

Look at the tiny bird
that has come by accident into the room:
for twenty heartbeats
it lay in a hand.
A human hand. Determined to protect.
Protective, owning nothing.
But
there on the window sill
free
it is still deep in terror,
strange to itself
and its surroundings,
the universe — no recognition.
Ah, how confusing a hand is,
even bent on rescue.
In the most helpful of hands
there is still death enough
and was money

VASE PAINTING

(*Supper of the Dead*)

Notice how our cups penetrate each other
without clinking. And wine passes through wine
like moonlight through its reflection
in the clouds. Oh quiet waning of the world . . .
and the clinking's delicate absence plays like a
butterfly with other butterflies
dancing around a warm stone.

Blind mouthfuls arch without the slightest
        coarseness,
feeding on nothing, in fact, like the amoeba,
even as I raise them closer to my lips,
I let each space remain just as it was:
and the only thing which can move me
is the dancer's step.

"WE ARE JUST MOUTH . . ."

We are just mouth. Who sings the distant heart
that lives whole and complete inside all things?
Its huge pulsations are divided up in us
into small pulsations. And its huge pain
is, like its huge joy, too much for us.
Therefore again and again we tear ourselves away
and are just mouth. But all at once
the huge heartbeat secretly breaks in on us,
so that we cry out — ,
and then are being, change, and face.

"OH, NOT TO BE EXCLUDED . . . "

Oh, not to be excluded,
not to be cut off
by such an insubstantial wall
from the measure of the stars.
Inner self, what is that?
If not a risen sky
through which birds are hurled, a sky
deep with the winds of return.

134

"NOW NOTHING CAN
PREVENT ME . . . "

Now nothing can prevent me
completing my appointed orbit — ,
it scares me to think a mortal could contain me.
A womb contained me once.
To break forth from it was fatal:
I broke forth into life. But are arms so deep,
are they fertile enough, to allow for
escape from them, through the first agony
of a new birth?

"NOW IT IS TIME THE GODS STEPPED OUT . . . "

Now it is time the gods stepped out
of everyday things . . .
Time they knocked down every wall
in my house. A new page. Only the wind,
caused by turning over such a page, would be
        enough
to shovel open the air as if it were earth:
a new breath-field. Oh gods, gods!
You frequent infiltrators, sleepers inside things,
who rise exulting, splashing
face and neck beside envisioned springs,
and who effortlessly add your being in repose
to what seemed filled already, our full life.
May it be your morning once again, gods.
We recur. You alone are origin.
The world rises with you, and beginning shines
through all the cracks of our failures . . .

"BIRDS' VOICES ARE STARTING TO PRAISE . . . "

Birds' voices are starting to praise.
And have a right to. We listen a long time.
(We're the ones in masks, oh God, and in
        costumes!)
What are they saying? a little insistence,
        a little sadness, and a lot of promise
which files away at the half-divulged future.
And in-between, in our hearing, heals
the beautiful silence they break.

LAST ENTRY

Come, you last of those I will see,
unutterable anguish interwoven with the flesh:
as I once burned in spirit, look, I burn
in you; the wood has held out a long time,
withheld its assent from the flames, but now
I'm burning in you, fueling you. Inside
your fury my accustomed quietude has turned
into a raging hell, unlike anything here.
Utterly pure, utterly, planlessly free of a future I
    climbed
the wild pyre of pain,
certain in this way of purchasing nothing to come
in exchange for this heart, whose reserves were
    exhausted.
Is that still me, burned beyond recognition?
I cannot gather my memories around me anymore.
Oh life, life: being outside. And I
in flames. No one recognizes me.

Resignation. This is not what illness was
once, in childhood. Respite. A secret way
to get bigger. Everything beckoning, whispering.
Don't confuse that first astonishment with this

NOTES

Improvisations of the Caprisian Winter. Capri, 1906-1907.

"To drink things dissolved and diluted . . ." Paris, September 1907.

Autumn Evening. Paris, end of September 1907.

The Sick Child. 1907-1908.

Walk at Night. Capri, April 17, 1908.

"Oh in childhood, God, how easy you were . . ." Paris, summer 1909.

"Haven't you known nights of love . . ." Paris, summer 1909.

To Lou Andreas-Salome. Duino, November-December 1911.

The Raising of Lazarus. Ronda, January 1913.

The Spanish Trilogy. Ronda, January 6-14, 1913.

"In ignorance before the heavens of my life . . ." Paris, early 1913.

Christ's Descent into Hell. Paris, April 1913.

"Abandoned in the mountains of the heart . . ." Irschenhausen, September 20, 1914.

To Benvenuta. Presumably: February 26, 1914, on the way from Paris to Berlin. For Magda von Hattinberg.

"The way water surfaces silently . . ." Irschenhausen, September 24-25, 1914. For Lulu Albert-Lazard.

Death. Munich, November 9, 1915.

Requiem on the Death of a Boy. Munich, November 13, 1915.

The Death of Moses. Verses 1-14: Paris, summer 1914; verses 15-22: Munich, October 1915.

The Lord's Words to John on Patmos. Munich, November 19-20, 1915. Inspired by Dürer's "Apocalypse."

Unfinished Elegy. Berg am Irschel, December 1920. Final stage of the draft.

The Hand. Probably: end of January, 1922, at Muzot.

Vase Painting (Supper of the Dead). Muzot, middle of February, 1922.

"We are just mouth . . ." Schöneck, end of September, 1923.

"Oh, not to be excluded . . ." Paris, summer 1925.

"Now nothing can prevent me . . ." Paris, summer 1925.

"Now it is time the gods stepped out . . ." Muzot, mid October, 1925.

"Birds' voices are starting to praise . . ." Val-Mont, mid March, 1926.

"Come, you last of those I will see . . ." Val-Mont, well into the middle of December, 1926: last entry in the last notebook.